Copyright © 2023 by Michael Jaynes (Author)

This book is protected by copyright law and is intended solely for personal use. Reproduction, distribution, or any other form of use requires the written permission of the author. The information presented in this book is for educational and entertainment purposes only, and while every effort has been made to ensure its accuracy and completeness, no guarantees are made. The author is not providing legal, financial, medical, or professional advice, and readers should consult with a licensed professional before implementing any of the techniques discussed in this book. The content in this book has been sourced from various reliable sources, but readers should exercise their own judgment when using this information. The author is not responsible for any losses, direct or indirect, that may occur from the use of this book, including but not limited to errors, omissions, or inaccuracies.

We hope this book has been informative and helpful on your journey to understanding and celebrating older adults. Thank you for your interest and support!

Title: The Art of Football Leadership

Subtitle: Insights from the World's Best Player-Managers

Series: Champions on and off the Field: The Success Stories of Footballers-Turned-Managers

By Michael Jaynes

"The coach is not the most important person in a football club. The most important person is the player."
Johan Cruyff, Dutch footballer and coach

"A football team is like a piano. You need eight men to carry it and three who can play the damn thing."
Bill Shankly, Liverpool FC manager

"I'm a bloody difficult man to work for because I'm always demanding. That's how you get on in life."
Sir Alex Ferguson, Manchester United

"The best coaches are like magicians. They can see what others can't see and make it happen."
Jose Mourinho, AS Roma FC manager.

"A football coach is not a dictator. He is someone who leads and inspires his players to achieve greatness."
Carlo Ancelotti, Real Madrid CF manager.

"I never expect my players to play a game that I wouldn't play myself."
Diego Simeone, Atletico Madrid FC manager

"The coach's role is to create an environment where players can be the best version of themselves."
Jurgen Klopp, Liverpool FC manager

"I am not a dictator, I am a coach."
Pep Guardiola, Manchester City FC manager

Table of Contents

Introduction 8
The importance of leadership and management in football 8
The difference between leadership and management 11
An overview of the book and its aims 14

Chapter 1: Roy Keane 16
Keane's playing career and leadership qualities 16
His approach to management and coaching 18
Case studies of his time at Sunderland and Ipswich Town 20
Lessons that can be learned from Keane's leadership style 23

Chapter 2: Rafael Benitez 26
Benitez's playing career and early coaching experience 26
His tactical innovations and attention to detail 29
Case studies of his time at Valencia, Liverpool, and Newcastle United 31
Lessons that can be learned from Benitez's management approach 34

Chapter 3: Marcelo Bielsa 37
Bielsa's philosophy of football and approach to management 37

His record of developing young players and creating successful teams *40*
Case studies of his time at Newell's Old Boys, Athletic Bilbao, and Leeds United *42*
Lessons that can be learned from Bielsa's leadership style *44*

Chapter 4: Emma Hayes 47

Hayes' playing career and early coaching experience ... *47*
Her approach to team building and player development *49*
Case studies of her time at Chelsea Women *52*
Lessons that can be learned from Hayes' management approach *55*

Chapter 5: Patrick Vieira 57

Vieira's playing career and leadership qualities *57*
His approach to management and player development *59*
Case studies of his time at New York City FC and OGC Nice *62*
Lessons that can be learned from Vieira's leadership style *66*

Chapter 6: Mauricio Pochettino 72

Pochettino's playing career and early coaching experience *72*
His approach to team building and player development *74*

Case studies of his time at Espanyol, Southampton, and Tottenham Hotspur 76

Lessons that can be learned from Pochettino's management approach 79

Chapter 7: Casey Stoney **82**

Stoney's playing career and early coaching experience . 82

Her approach to team building and player development 86

Case studies of her time at Manchester United Women . 88

Lessons that can be learned from Stoney's management approach 91

Conclusion **94**

The key qualities of successful football leaders and managers 94

The importance of adaptability and innovation in modern football 97

Final thoughts and recommendations for aspiring managers and coaches 100

Key Terms and Definitions **104**

Supporting Materials **106**

Introduction
The importance of leadership and management in football

Football is a sport that requires a combination of physical prowess, mental acuity, and strategic planning. While players are often the ones in the spotlight, the success of a team ultimately relies on the leadership and management skills of its coaches and managers. The importance of leadership and management in football cannot be overstated, as it can make the difference between a mediocre team and a championship-winning one.

In this book, we will explore the qualities that make great football leaders and managers, using successful player-managers as case studies. By examining the careers of Roy Keane, Rafael Benitez, Marcelo Bielsa, Emma Hayes, Patrick Vieira, Mauricio Pochettino, and Casey Stoney, we will gain insights into what it takes to succeed in the world of football management.

The importance of leadership and management in football:

Leadership and management are critical components of any successful football team. While there is often overlap between the two, leadership generally refers to the ability to inspire and motivate others, while management involves the more practical aspects of organizing and coordinating a team.

In football, leadership is essential for setting the tone and creating a positive team culture. A great leader can inspire their players to work harder, strive for excellence, and develop a sense of camaraderie and unity. They can also instill a winning mentality and ensure that everyone is working towards a common goal.

On the other hand, management is necessary for ensuring that the team is organized and efficient. A great manager can coordinate team training and practice sessions, develop strategies for games, and make tactical adjustments during matches. They can also oversee player development and ensure that everyone is working towards their full potential.

However, leadership and management are not mutually exclusive. A great football manager must possess both qualities to succeed. They must be able to inspire their players, while also managing the practical aspects of running a team. This requires a delicate balance between motivating players and making strategic decisions that will ultimately lead to success.

Additionally, effective leadership and management can have a positive impact on the performance of individual players. When players feel valued and supported by their leaders, they are more likely to perform at their best. They are also more likely to be motivated to work harder and improve their skills.

In conclusion, leadership and management are critical components of any successful football team. Without effective leadership and management, even the most talented players will struggle to achieve success. By examining the careers of successful player-managers, we can gain insights into what it takes to become a great leader and manager in the world of football.

The difference between leadership and management

Leadership and management are two terms that are often used interchangeably, but they are actually distinct concepts. While both are important for the success of a football team, it is important to understand the differences between the two. In this chapter, we will explore the difference between leadership and management, and how they both play a role in the world of football.

Leadership and management are often seen as two sides of the same coin, but they are actually quite different. Leadership is focused on inspiring and motivating others to achieve a common goal, while management is focused on organizing and coordinating resources to achieve that goal.

In football, leadership is essential for setting the tone and creating a positive team culture. A great leader can inspire their players to work harder, strive for excellence, and develop a sense of camaraderie and unity. They can also instill a winning mentality and ensure that everyone is working towards a common goal.

On the other hand, management is necessary for ensuring that the team is organized and efficient. A great manager can coordinate team training and practice sessions, develop strategies for games, and make tactical adjustments during matches. They can also oversee player development and ensure that everyone is working towards their full potential.

The main difference between leadership and management is that leadership is focused on people, while management is focused on tasks. A leader is someone who can inspire and motivate others, while a manager is someone who can organize and coordinate resources to achieve a goal.

Another important difference between leadership and management is their approach to decision-making. Leaders are often more intuitive and rely on their instincts to make decisions, while managers are more analytical and use data and information to make decisions.

In football, both leadership and management are necessary for the success of a team. A great leader can inspire their players to work harder and achieve success, while a great manager can ensure that the team is organized and efficient. The best football managers are those who can balance both leadership and management skills, and use them effectively to achieve success.

Conclusion:

While leadership and management are often used interchangeably, they are actually distinct concepts that play different roles in the world of football. Leadership is focused on inspiring and motivating others to achieve a common goal, while management is focused on organizing and coordinating resources to achieve that goal. Both are necessary for the success of a football team, and the best managers are those who can balance both skills effectively. By understanding the difference between leadership and management, aspiring football managers can develop the skills necessary to lead their team to success.

An overview of the book and its aims

"The Art of Football Leadership" is divided into seven chapters, each focusing on a different player-manager. The book covers a range of different leadership styles, from Roy Keane's no-nonsense approach to Marcelo Bielsa's innovative philosophy of football. Each chapter includes case studies of the manager's time at different clubs, as well as lessons that can be learned from their leadership style.

The book is aimed at aspiring football managers and coaches who want to develop their leadership and management skills. By examining the qualities and skills that have made these successful player-managers, the book provides insights and practical advice that can be applied to any football team or organization.

The aims of the book:

The main aim of "The Art of Football Leadership" is to provide insights into what makes a great football leader and manager. By examining the careers of some of the world's best player-managers, the book aims to identify the key qualities and skills that have made them successful both on and off the pitch.

Another aim of the book is to provide practical advice and guidance for aspiring football managers and coaches. By examining case studies of different player-managers, the book aims to provide insights into how to develop a successful leadership style, how to motivate and inspire players, and how to manage resources effectively.

Finally, the book aims to highlight the importance of adaptability and innovation in modern football. As the game continues to evolve, successful managers are those who can adapt to new challenges and implement innovative strategies to stay ahead of the game. By examining the careers of some of the world's best player-managers, the book aims to provide examples of how to stay ahead of the curve and succeed in a rapidly changing football landscape.

Conclusion:

"The Art of Football Leadership" is a book that provides insights into what makes a great football leader and manager. By examining the careers of some of the world's best player-managers, the book aims to identify the key qualities and skills that have made them successful both on and off the pitch. It also provides practical advice and guidance for aspiring football managers and coaches, and highlights the importance of adaptability and innovation in modern football. Whether you are an aspiring manager or a seasoned pro, "The Art of Football Leadership" is a valuable resource for anyone looking to develop their leadership and management skills in the world of football.

Chapter 1: Roy Keane

Keane's playing career and leadership qualities

Roy Keane is widely regarded as one of the greatest captains in the history of football. He is known for his fierce competitiveness, his no-nonsense approach to the game, and his unwavering commitment to his team. Keane played for some of the biggest clubs in the world, including Manchester United, Celtic, and Nottingham Forest, and he also captained the Republic of Ireland national team.

Keane's playing career was marked by his exceptional leadership qualities. He was a natural leader on the pitch, and he had an incredible ability to motivate and inspire his teammates. Keane was not afraid to speak his mind and he would often challenge his teammates if he felt they were not giving their best effort. He was also known for his tough tackling and aggressive playing style, which made him an imposing presence on the pitch.

Perhaps the most famous example of Keane's leadership came during Manchester United's 1999 Champions League campaign. In the semi-final second leg against Juventus, United found themselves 2-0 down after just 11 minutes. Keane rallied his teammates, scored a goal himself, and played a key role in leading United to a famous comeback victory. After the match, his manager Sir Alex

Ferguson famously remarked that Keane had "dragged us back from the dead."

Off the pitch, Keane was also known for his leadership qualities. He was a strong presence in the dressing room and was respected by all of his teammates. He would often take younger players under his wing and help them to develop their skills and confidence. Keane was also known for his work ethic and dedication to training, which set an example for his teammates to follow.

Keane's leadership qualities were not without controversy, however. He was known for his fiery temper and would often clash with referees and opponents on the pitch. He was also involved in a number of high-profile incidents, including a physical altercation with Alf-Inge Haaland which resulted in a long-term injury for the Norwegian player.

Despite these controversies, Keane's leadership qualities were widely admired by his teammates and opponents alike. He was a natural leader who inspired those around him and led by example on and off the pitch. In his later career, Keane transitioned into coaching and management, where he continued to demonstrate his leadership qualities and inspire his teams to success.

His approach to management and coaching

Roy Keane is known for his leadership qualities and his approach to management and coaching. Keane's playing career, which was marked by his passion, intensity, and discipline, provided him with a solid foundation for his later roles as a manager and coach. Keane was a natural leader on the pitch, and he brought those same qualities to his management and coaching roles.

Keane's approach to management and coaching is characterized by his intensity, his attention to detail, and his focus on discipline and hard work. Keane is known for his no-nonsense style and his ability to motivate his players to perform at their best. He demands a high level of commitment from his players, and he is not afraid to call them out if they are not meeting his standards.

One of the key aspects of Keane's approach to management and coaching is his focus on preparation. Keane believes that success in football is achieved through hard work and preparation, and he is meticulous in his approach to both. He spends a lot of time analyzing his opponents and developing game plans to exploit their weaknesses. He also works closely with his players to ensure that they are physically and mentally prepared for every match.

Another aspect of Keane's approach to management and coaching is his emphasis on discipline and accountability. Keane believes that success is achieved through hard work and discipline, and he expects his players to be disciplined both on and off the pitch. He is known for his strict training regimes, which are designed to improve his players' physical and mental toughness.

Finally, Keane's approach to management and coaching is characterized by his ability to build strong relationships with his players. Keane is known for his loyalty and his commitment to his players, and he works hard to build trust and respect with each of them. He is also a good communicator, and he is able to convey his ideas and expectations clearly to his players.

In summary, Roy Keane's approach to management and coaching is characterized by his intensity, his attention to detail, his focus on discipline and hard work, and his ability to build strong relationships with his players. These qualities have enabled him to achieve success both as a player and as a manager, and they offer valuable insights into what it takes to be a successful leader in football.

Case studies of his time at Sunderland and Ipswich Town

Roy Keane's time at Sunderland and Ipswich Town provides valuable insights into his approach to management and coaching.

After a brief stint as an assistant manager at Celtic, Keane took over as manager of Sunderland in 2006. At the time, Sunderland was languishing in the bottom half of the Championship, but Keane's arrival heralded a new era of success for the club. In his first season in charge, Keane led Sunderland to the Championship title and promotion to the Premier League.

One of Keane's key strengths as a manager was his ability to create a sense of discipline and accountability within the squad. He was known for his strict training regimes and his uncompromising attitude towards players who didn't meet his high standards. At Sunderland, he famously fined several players for arriving late to training, including star striker Dwight Yorke.

Keane also had a shrewd eye for talent and was able to assemble a squad of players who complemented each other's strengths. He signed several players who would go on to become key members of the Sunderland team, including goalkeeper Craig Gordon, midfielder Kieran Richardson, and striker Kenwyne Jones.

However, Keane's time at Sunderland was not without its challenges. He clashed with the club's owner, Ellis Short, over transfer funds and was ultimately sacked in 2008 after a poor run of results in the Premier League.

Keane's next managerial role came at Ipswich Town, where he took over in 2009. However, his time at Ipswich was less successful than his spell at Sunderland. Despite signing several high-profile players, including Jimmy Bullard and Lee Bowyer, Keane was unable to lead Ipswich to promotion from the Championship and was sacked in January 2011.

One of the reasons for Keane's struggles at Ipswich was his tendency to fall out with players and staff members. He was involved in several high-profile arguments with players, including striker Tamas Priskin and goalkeeper Brian Murphy, and his abrasive management style often created a tense atmosphere within the squad.

Overall, Keane's time at Sunderland and Ipswich provides a fascinating case study of a manager who was able to achieve great success through his tough, no-nonsense approach to management. However, his struggles at Ipswich also highlight the importance of building strong relationships with players and staff members, and the dangers of creating a confrontational atmosphere within the squad.

Lessons that can be learned from Keane's leadership style

Roy Keane is a prime example of a footballer who became a successful manager, and his leadership style offers several valuable lessons for aspiring coaches and managers.

One of the key lessons that can be learned from Keane's leadership style is the importance of honesty and transparency. Keane was known for his no-nonsense approach to management, and he was never afraid to tell his players what he thought. This honesty helped to build trust and respect between Keane and his players, which in turn allowed him to get the best out of them.

Another lesson that can be learned from Keane's leadership style is the importance of setting high standards. Keane was a perfectionist on the pitch, and he brought this same level of intensity to his managerial role. He demanded the best from his players, both in training and on match days, and he was not afraid to call out those who failed to meet his expectations. This focus on high standards helped to create a culture of excellence within his teams.

Keane was also a master of man-management, and he understood the importance of building relationships with his players. He was known for his ability to get the best out of individual players, and he was skilled at identifying their strengths and weaknesses. This allowed him to tailor his coaching style to suit each individual, which in turn helped to improve their performance on the pitch.

Another key lesson that can be learned from Keane's leadership style is the importance of taking responsibility for your own mistakes. Keane was famously sent home from the 2002 World Cup after he criticized his teammates in an interview. However, he later admitted that he was wrong to do so, and he took full responsibility for his actions. This willingness to admit when you are wrong is a crucial part of effective leadership, as it helps to build trust and respect among team members.

Finally, Keane's leadership style also highlights the importance of having a clear vision and a strong sense of purpose. Keane was always driven by a desire to win, and he instilled this same sense of purpose in his players. He was able to articulate his vision for the team, and he worked tirelessly to ensure that everyone was aligned with this vision. This sense of purpose helped to motivate his players and to create a culture of success within his teams.

Overall, Roy Keane's leadership style offers several valuable lessons for aspiring coaches and managers. His honesty, focus on high standards, man-management skills, willingness to take responsibility, and clear sense of purpose are all qualities that are essential for effective leadership in any context.

Chapter 2: Rafael Benitez

Benitez's playing career and early coaching experience

Rafael Benitez is a former Spanish football player and coach who has made significant contributions to the sport. Benitez played as a defensive midfielder for several teams in the Spanish league, including Real Madrid Castilla, CD Linares, and CD Parla. Although his playing career was not particularly remarkable, he quickly discovered his passion for coaching and began building his reputation as a coach early on.

After retiring from playing in 1986, Benitez began working as a youth coach at Real Madrid. He spent several years coaching the youth teams and gradually worked his way up the ranks to become an assistant coach for the first team. In 1995, he was offered his first head coaching job at Real Valladolid. He spent one season with the team before moving to Osasuna, where he led the team to promotion to La Liga for the first time in over a decade.

Benitez's success at Osasuna caught the attention of Tenerife, and he was hired as the team's head coach in 2000. In his first season with the team, he led them to a fifth-place finish in La Liga, their highest ever finish. Benitez's tactical acumen and attention to detail were beginning to gain widespread recognition, and it wasn't long before he was offered a job with one of Spain's biggest clubs, Valencia.

Benitez was appointed as Valencia's head coach in 2001, and he quickly transformed the team into one of the best in Europe. In his first season with the team, he led them to victory in the UEFA Cup, and the following season he won La Liga. Valencia's success under Benitez was due in large part to his innovative tactical approach, which involved a strong focus on defensive solidity and efficient counter-attacking football.

Benitez's success at Valencia led to him being appointed as Liverpool's head coach in 2004. His time at Liverpool is perhaps best remembered for the team's remarkable comeback in the 2005 Champions League final against AC Milan, in which they overturned a three-goal deficit to win the trophy. Benitez's tactical acumen and ability to motivate his players were key factors in the team's success, and he quickly became a fan favorite at Anfield.

Overall, Benitez's playing career was relatively modest, but he quickly established himself as one of the most innovative and successful coaches in world football. His attention to detail and tactical acumen have been the hallmarks of his coaching career, and he has consistently demonstrated an ability to get the best out of his players. As we will see in the following chapters, his success as a coach has been built on a foundation of strong leadership skills and a deep understanding of the game.

His tactical innovations and attention to detail

Rafael Benitez's tactical innovations and attention to detail have been a hallmark of his management career. Throughout his career, he has been praised for his ability to adapt his tactics to different opponents and situations. His tactical approach has been shaped by his early experiences as a coach in the Spanish lower leagues.

One of Benitez's most significant tactical innovations was the use of the 4-2-3-1 formation, which he first used at Valencia. This formation allowed him to get the best out of his attacking players, while also providing defensive stability. The system was based on two holding midfielders, who provided cover for the defense while also allowing the attacking players to push forward.

Another important aspect of Benitez's tactical approach is his attention to detail. He is known for his meticulous preparation for matches, analyzing opponents' strengths and weaknesses in great detail. He leaves no stone unturned in his preparation, studying videos of opponents' matches and analyzing statistics to gain an edge.

Benitez's attention to detail extends to training sessions as well. He is known for his rigorous training sessions, which focus on developing players' skills and improving their fitness levels. His training sessions are designed to simulate game situations and help players improve their decision-making abilities.

In addition to his tactical innovations and attention to detail, Benitez is also known for his ability to motivate his players. He has a reputation for being a demanding coach who pushes his players to perform at their best. His ability to motivate his players has been a key factor in his success, as he has been able to get the best out of teams with limited resources.

Overall, Benitez's tactical innovations and attention to detail have been a major factor in his success as a manager. His ability to adapt his tactics to different opponents and situations has been crucial in his success, while his attention to detail and rigorous training sessions have helped to develop his players' skills and improve their fitness levels.

Case studies of his time at Valencia, Liverpool, and Newcastle United

Rafael Benitez is widely recognized as one of the most innovative and tactically astute managers in the modern game. His approach to management is characterized by his meticulous attention to detail, and his ability to adapt his tactics and strategies to the strengths and weaknesses of his opponents. In this chapter, we will examine some of the key moments from Benitez's managerial career, including his time at Valencia, Liverpool, and Newcastle United.

Valencia (2001-2004) Benitez's first major managerial role was at Valencia, where he took over in 2001. In his first season in charge, he led the club to a third-place finish in La Liga and a UEFA Cup win. The following season, he won the La Liga title, breaking the duopoly of Real Madrid and Barcelona for the first time in a decade.

One of the keys to Benitez's success at Valencia was his tactical flexibility. He was able to switch between a 4-4-2, a 4-2-3-1, and a 4-3-3 depending on the opposition. His team was also known for their organized defense, which conceded just 27 goals in the 2003-04 La Liga season.

Liverpool (2004-2010) After his success at Valencia, Benitez was appointed as the manager of Liverpool in 2004. He quickly set about rebuilding the squad, bringing in players such as Xabi Alonso and Luis Garcia. In his first season in charge, he led the club to a dramatic Champions League triumph, coming back from 3-0 down to beat AC Milan on penalties in the final.

One of Benitez's most famous tactical innovations during his time at Liverpool was the use of a diamond midfield. This formation allowed him to play both Steven Gerrard and Xabi Alonso in central midfield, while also providing defensive cover through Javier Mascherano. The diamond midfield was particularly effective in the 2008-09 season, when Liverpool finished runners-up in the Premier League.

Newcastle United (2016-2019) Benitez took charge of Newcastle United in 2016, and immediately set about stabilizing the club after their relegation to the Championship. In his first full season in charge, he led the club back to the Premier League as champions of the Championship.

One of the hallmarks of Benitez's time at Newcastle was his ability to get the best out of his players. He was particularly effective in motivating players who had struggled under previous managers, such as Jonjo Shelvey and Dwight Gayle. Benitez was also praised for his tactical flexibility, using a variety of formations depending on the opposition.

Overall, Benitez's time at Valencia, Liverpool, and Newcastle United demonstrates his ability to adapt his tactics and strategies to the strengths and weaknesses of his opponents. His attention to detail and tactical innovations have made him one of the most successful managers of his generation, and there are many lessons that aspiring managers can learn from his approach to the game.

Lessons that can be learned from Benitez's management approach

Rafael Benitez's management approach is known for its tactical innovations, attention to detail, and ability to create successful teams even with limited resources. Here are some lessons that aspiring managers and coaches can learn from Benitez's approach:

1. Tactical flexibility: One of Benitez's strengths is his ability to adapt his tactics to suit the strengths and weaknesses of his players and opponents. He is known for his attention to detail and spends a lot of time analyzing the opposition before matches to identify potential weaknesses that his team can exploit. This ability to adapt and make changes during a match can be crucial in achieving success.

2. Attention to detail: Benitez is known for his meticulous attention to detail, both on and off the pitch. He spends a lot of time studying video footage of his team's matches and training sessions to identify areas for improvement. He also pays attention to the small details, such as players' diets and hydration levels, to ensure that they are in optimal physical condition.

3. The importance of squad rotation: Benitez is a firm believer in squad rotation, especially when playing in multiple competitions. He believes that keeping players fresh

and avoiding injuries is key to maintaining a successful season. This approach can also help to keep the squad motivated and engaged throughout the season.

4. Man-management skills: Benitez is known for his excellent man-management skills, which have helped him to get the best out of his players. He is able to motivate and inspire his players, and also has a good understanding of how to deal with different personalities within the squad.

5. Building a strong team spirit: Benitez places a strong emphasis on team spirit and unity. He believes that a cohesive team is more important than individual talent, and works hard to build a positive team culture. This can help to create a strong sense of camaraderie within the squad, and can be crucial in achieving success on the pitch.

6. Effective use of resources: Benitez has achieved success with a variety of clubs, including some with limited resources. He is adept at getting the best out of the resources available to him, whether that means developing young players or making astute signings within a limited budget. This ability to work effectively within financial constraints can be a valuable skill for any manager.

7. Continuous improvement: Finally, Benitez is known for his relentless focus on continuous improvement. He is always looking for ways to improve his team, whether that

means developing new tactics, improving training methods, or making adjustments to the squad. This approach can help to keep a team moving forward and can be crucial in maintaining success over the long term.

In summary, Rafael Benitez's management approach is characterized by tactical flexibility, attention to detail, effective man-management skills, and a relentless focus on continuous improvement. Aspiring managers and coaches can learn valuable lessons from his approach, which has helped him to achieve success at the highest level of the game.

Chapter 3: Marcelo Bielsa
Bielsa's philosophy of football and approach to management

Marcelo Bielsa is a legendary figure in the world of football management, known for his unique and innovative approach to the game. Bielsa, who is from Argentina, has managed some of the biggest clubs in South America and Europe, and has had a profound influence on the sport through his philosophy and tactics.

One of Bielsa's most defining traits is his intense focus on the game itself. He is known for his meticulous preparation, and often spends hours analyzing video footage and scouting reports in order to develop a detailed game plan for each match. This attention to detail extends to all aspects of his management, from training sessions to player recruitment.

At the heart of Bielsa's approach to management is his philosophy of football. He believes that the game should be played with an emphasis on attacking play and high intensity, and that every player on the team should be willing to work hard both on and off the ball. This philosophy is based on the idea that football should be a beautiful and exciting game, rather than simply a means of winning.

One of the key principles of Bielsa's philosophy is the idea of positional play. This involves organizing the team into specific positions on the field, with each player having a clearly defined role and set of responsibilities. This approach allows Bielsa to control the flow of the game and create scoring opportunities, while also minimizing the risk of conceding goals.

Another key aspect of Bielsa's approach to management is his emphasis on physical fitness. He believes that in order to play his high-intensity style of football, players must be in peak physical condition. As a result, he places a strong emphasis on fitness training and conditioning, and expects his players to maintain a high level of fitness throughout the season.

In terms of tactics, Bielsa is known for his use of a high press. This involves pressing the opposition high up the pitch in order to win the ball back quickly and create scoring opportunities. This tactic can be very effective when executed properly, but it requires a high level of fitness and discipline from the players.

Bielsa's approach to management has been hugely influential in the world of football, and has inspired many other coaches and managers to adopt similar philosophies and tactics. His innovative ideas and attention to detail have helped to shape the way the game is played today, and his legacy will continue to be felt for many years to come.

His record of developing young players and creating successful teams

Marcelo Bielsa is widely regarded as one of the most innovative and influential coaches in modern football. His unique philosophy and approach to management have led to success at both club and international level, and he has developed a reputation for developing young players and creating successful teams.

Bielsa's focus on player development and tactical innovation is evident throughout his career. He has often been described as a perfectionist, with a relentless attention to detail that extends to every aspect of his team's preparation and performance. Bielsa's philosophy is centered around the idea of attacking football, where every player on the pitch is expected to contribute to both the defensive and attacking phases of play.

One of the most impressive aspects of Bielsa's management style is his ability to develop young players. He is known for his commitment to youth development and has a reputation for spotting talent and nurturing it to its full potential. Bielsa's approach to player development involves a focus on technical skills, physical fitness, and mental toughness. He places great importance on the role of the coach in shaping the player's character, and his methods have been credited with producing a number of successful footballers.

Bielsa's record of success speaks for itself. During his time as coach of the Chile national team, he led the team to its first ever World Cup knockout stage appearance, and also won the Copa America in 2015. At club level, he has had successful stints with Newell's Old Boys, Velez Sarsfield, Athletic Bilbao, Lille, and most recently, Leeds United.

One of Bielsa's most notable achievements has been his work with Leeds United. After taking over in 2018, Bielsa quickly transformed the team's fortunes, leading them to promotion to the Premier League in his second season. His tactical innovations and player development methods were instrumental in achieving this success, and his influence on the club is still felt to this day.

There are a number of lessons that can be learned from Bielsa's management style. His commitment to player development, tactical innovation, and attention to detail are all qualities that can be emulated by other coaches. Bielsa's focus on attacking football and player development have been particularly successful, and these ideas can be adapted to suit other teams and leagues. Overall, Bielsa's approach to football management is a unique and inspiring example of what can be achieved through dedication and hard work.

Case studies of his time at Newell's Old Boys, Athletic Bilbao, and Leeds United

Marcelo Bielsa is a renowned manager known for his unique approach to the game of football. His success has come from his ability to develop young players and create successful teams with limited resources. This chapter will explore some of the case studies of his time at Newell's Old Boys, Athletic Bilbao, and Leeds United, showcasing his management style and the impact he had on these clubs.

Newell's Old Boys: Bielsa's career as a manager began at Newell's Old Boys in 1990. In his first season, he led the team to win the Primera Division and was subsequently named Coach of the Year in Argentina. Bielsa built a team that was both defensively solid and lethal in attack. He also introduced a high pressing game that helped his team win possession quickly and effectively.

Athletic Bilbao: In 2011, Bielsa was appointed as the head coach of Athletic Bilbao. Bielsa took Bilbao to the Europa League final in his first season, where they were eventually defeated by Atletico Madrid. However, his impact was felt throughout the season, with the team playing a fast-paced, attacking brand of football that was enjoyable to watch. Bielsa also introduced an intense physical training regime that was focused on improving the players' fitness levels.

Leeds United: Bielsa's current managerial job is at Leeds United. He was appointed as the head coach in 2018 and led the team to win the Championship in his second season, gaining promotion to the Premier League. Bielsa's arrival at Leeds United has seen the team undergo a transformation, both on and off the pitch. He has introduced a high-intensity pressing game, which has seen the team win possession quickly and create more scoring opportunities. Bielsa's training methods are also rigorous, with sessions often lasting several hours.

Lessons learned: Bielsa's case studies show that he is a manager who is willing to innovate and take risks. His approach to management is focused on developing young players and creating a team that plays an attacking, high-intensity game. Bielsa's methods also show that he is a manager who is not afraid to challenge established norms and introduce new ideas. Finally, Bielsa is a manager who understands the importance of hard work and dedication, both on and off the pitch. His rigorous training methods have helped his teams achieve success, and his focus on fitness and conditioning has allowed his teams to maintain a high level of performance throughout the season.

Lessons that can be learned from Bielsa's leadership style

Marcelo Bielsa is widely regarded as one of the most innovative and influential coaches in modern football. His approach to leadership and management has produced impressive results throughout his career, and there are several lessons that can be learned from his leadership style.

1. Attention to Detail: One of the key aspects of Bielsa's approach is his attention to detail. He is known for his meticulous preparation, studying opposition teams extensively and creating detailed game plans. This level of preparation enables his teams to have a clear understanding of their roles and responsibilities, and to execute their game plan with precision.

2. Emphasis on Teamwork: Bielsa's management style is characterized by a strong emphasis on teamwork. He creates a cohesive team environment where players are encouraged to work together and support each other. This approach has been particularly successful in developing young players, who benefit from a positive and nurturing environment.

3. High Standards: Bielsa has high standards for his players and staff, and he expects nothing less than their best effort. He is not afraid to hold players accountable for their

performance, but he does so in a constructive and supportive manner. This creates a culture of accountability and responsibility, which can be key to success at the highest level of competition.

4. Continuous Improvement: Another key aspect of Bielsa's leadership style is his commitment to continuous improvement. He encourages his players to learn from their mistakes and to strive for constant improvement. This approach has been successful in developing players who are not only technically skilled, but also mentally tough and adaptable.

5. Clear Communication: Bielsa places a strong emphasis on clear communication, both on and off the field. He uses video analysis extensively to help players understand their performance and to identify areas for improvement. He also communicates his expectations clearly to his players and staff, ensuring that everyone is on the same page.

In conclusion, Marcelo Bielsa's leadership style is characterized by attention to detail, emphasis on teamwork, high standards, continuous improvement, and clear communication. These qualities have enabled him to create successful teams and develop young players throughout his career. By studying and learning from his approach, leaders in any field can gain valuable insights into effective management and leadership.

Chapter 4: Emma Hayes

Hayes' playing career and early coaching experience

Emma Hayes is one of the most successful and respected women's football coaches in the world. Her journey to becoming a top-class coach was not easy, and her playing career played an important role in shaping her leadership style.

Hayes started playing football when she was a child, and she quickly fell in love with the game. She played for several teams in her youth, including Millwall Lionesses, where she won two league titles. However, her playing career was cut short by a knee injury, and she had to retire from the game at the age of 24.

After her retirement, Hayes turned to coaching and began working with the Arsenal women's team as a community coach. She quickly rose through the ranks and was eventually appointed as the head coach of the team in 2006.

Hayes' early coaching experience was heavily influenced by her playing career. She understood the importance of building strong relationships with her players and creating a positive team culture. She also believed in the importance of discipline and hard work, and she was not afraid to be tough when she needed to be.

Under Hayes' leadership, Arsenal won the Women's Premier League Cup and the UEFA Women's Cup. However, despite her success, she felt that she needed to continue learning and developing as a coach. In 2011, she left Arsenal to take up a coaching role at the United States' club Chicago Red Stars.

Her time at Chicago was brief, and in 2012 she returned to England to take up the role of manager at Chelsea women's team. She had a tough start at Chelsea, but she quickly turned the team's fortunes around. Under her leadership, Chelsea won several domestic and international titles, including the Women's Super League, the Women's FA Cup, and the UEFA Women's Champions League.

Hayes' playing career and early coaching experience played a critical role in shaping her leadership style. She was tough but fair, disciplined but supportive, and focused on building strong relationships with her players. Her success at Chelsea is a testament to her leadership skills, and she is now considered one of the best women's football coaches in the world.

Her approach to team building and player development

Emma Hayes is a highly respected manager in women's football, having guided Chelsea Women to numerous domestic and European successes. One of her greatest strengths is her ability to build strong teams and develop players, and in this chapter, we will explore her approach to team building and player development.

Building a strong team

One of the first things that Hayes does when building a team is to create a positive team culture. She believes that having a strong team culture is essential for success, as it helps to create a sense of belonging and unity within the team. To create this culture, she focuses on building relationships between players, as well as between players and staff. She encourages her players to be themselves and to express their personalities, which helps to create a relaxed and supportive environment.

Another key element of Hayes' approach to team building is her emphasis on communication. She believes that open and honest communication is essential for creating a high-performing team, as it helps to build trust and understanding between players and staff. She encourages her players to communicate with each other both on and off the pitch, and also encourages them to communicate with the coaching staff about their needs and concerns.

Player development

Hayes is also highly focused on player development, and is known for her ability to develop young players into top-class professionals. One of the key ways in which she does this is by creating a challenging and stimulating training environment. She believes that players learn best when they are challenged, and so she sets high standards in training and expects her players to push themselves to improve.

Another important element of Hayes' approach to player development is her focus on individualized coaching. She recognizes that each player is unique and has their own strengths and weaknesses, and so she tailors her coaching to each individual player. She also encourages her players to take responsibility for their own development, and works with them to create individual development plans.

Hayes also places a strong emphasis on creating a positive and supportive environment for her players. She believes that players perform best when they feel valued and supported, and so she works hard to create a culture of support and encouragement within the team. This includes providing emotional support to players when they are struggling, as well as creating opportunities for players to socialize and build relationships off the pitch.

Conclusion

Emma Hayes' approach to team building and player development is highly effective, as evidenced by her impressive record of success with Chelsea Women. By creating a positive team culture, emphasizing communication, and focusing on individualized coaching and player development, she is able to build high-performing teams and develop young players into top-class professionals. Her emphasis on creating a supportive and positive environment also helps to ensure that her players are happy and motivated, which in turn contributes to their success on the pitch.

Case studies of her time at Chelsea Women

Emma Hayes is one of the most successful managers in women's football history, and her time at Chelsea Women has been marked by a number of impressive achievements. In this chapter, we will take a closer look at some of the key moments and matches that have defined Hayes' tenure at the club.

1. Winning the Double in 2015

Emma Hayes arrived at Chelsea Women in 2012, and it took her three years to build a team capable of challenging for major honours. In 2015, Chelsea Women won the FA Women's Cup and the Women's Super League, becoming the first English club to win the Double in women's football.

The team's success was built on a solid defence, with Hayes deploying a back three system that allowed her full-backs to push forward and support the attack. At the heart of the defence was the experienced duo of Gilly Flaherty and Niamh Fahey, while up front, the goals were shared between the likes of Eniola Aluko, Fran Kirby, and Ji So-yun.

The Double was a historic achievement for Chelsea Women, and it marked the beginning of a new era of dominance in English women's football.

2. Champions League success in 2021

After several years of near misses and disappointments, Emma Hayes and Chelsea Women finally reached the pinnacle of European football in 2021, winning the Champions League for the first time in the club's history.

The final against Barcelona was a masterclass in tactical planning and execution, with Hayes deploying a high-pressing system that disrupted Barcelona's possession-based game. The goals came from the likes of Sam Kerr and Fran Kirby, who were a constant menace to the Barcelona defence.

Hayes' ability to get the best out of her players was evident throughout the campaign, with Chelsea Women winning 11 of their 12 matches en route to the final. The triumph was a fitting reward for Hayes' hard work and dedication, and it cemented her status as one of the most successful managers in the women's game.

3. Development of young players

One of the hallmarks of Emma Hayes' time at Chelsea Women has been her commitment to developing young players. The likes of Fran Kirby, Erin Cuthbert, and Bethany England have all flourished under her guidance, becoming key members of the team and earning international recognition.

Hayes' philosophy of giving youth a chance has paid dividends both on and off the pitch, with many of the club's young players becoming role models for the next generation of female footballers.

4. Building a winning culture

Finally, Emma Hayes has been instrumental in building a winning culture at Chelsea Women. She has instilled a belief and a confidence in her players that has allowed them to compete at the highest level and achieve great things.

Hayes' attention to detail and her ability to get the best out of her players have been key factors in this success. She has created an environment where everyone is committed to the same goal, and where hard work and determination are the norm.

Lessons learned:

- The importance of patience and long-term planning in building a successful team

- The value of tactical flexibility and the ability to adapt to different opponents and situations

- The benefits of investing in young players and giving them opportunities to develop and succeed

- The importance of creating a winning culture and instilling a sense of belief and confidence in the team.

Lessons that can be learned from Hayes' management approach

Emma Hayes is a highly regarded manager in women's football, having led Chelsea Women to numerous titles and international success. Her leadership approach has been widely praised, and there are several valuable lessons that can be learned from her management style.

One key lesson is the importance of developing a strong team culture. Hayes has emphasized the need for her players to feel like they are part of a family, and she has worked hard to create a positive and supportive environment within the team. This has helped to foster a strong sense of togetherness and has enabled the players to perform at their best.

Another lesson is the value of player development. Hayes has a reputation for being an excellent coach, and she has helped to develop several top players during her time at Chelsea Women. She has also shown a willingness to give young players a chance to prove themselves, which has helped to create a culture of growth and development within the team.

Hayes is also known for her tactical flexibility. She has a strong understanding of the game and is not afraid to make bold decisions in order to win matches. This has helped her team to achieve success both domestically and internationally.

In addition to these specific lessons, Hayes' management style is characterized by a number of broader qualities that are worth emulating. She is a highly motivated and hard-working individual who sets high standards for herself and her team. She is also a good communicator, able to motivate and inspire her players to perform at their best.

Overall, there is much that can be learned from Emma Hayes' approach to management. Her emphasis on team culture, player development, tactical flexibility, and personal qualities such as motivation and communication make her a valuable role model for aspiring coaches and managers in women's football and beyond.

Chapter 5: Patrick Vieira

Vieira's playing career and leadership qualities

Patrick Vieira is one of the most iconic footballers of his generation, and his career as a player is often cited as a prime example of leadership on and off the field. Born in Dakar, Senegal, Vieira moved to France at a young age and began playing football in his teens. He quickly caught the attention of scouts, and was eventually signed by AS Cannes, a French club, in 1993.

Vieira's playing style was marked by his physical presence, his technical skill, and his tactical intelligence. He was known for his ability to read the game and anticipate his opponents' moves, and he was equally comfortable playing in a defensive or an attacking role. He quickly established himself as a key player for AS Cannes, and his performances earned him a move to AC Milan in 1995.

Vieira's time at Milan was relatively brief, and he struggled to establish himself in the team. However, his fortunes changed when he moved to Arsenal in 1996. Under the guidance of manager Arsène Wenger, Vieira began to flourish, and he quickly became one of the most important players in the team. Over the course of his nine seasons at Arsenal, Vieira won three Premier League titles and four FA

Cups, and he was widely regarded as one of the best midfielders in the world.

Vieira's leadership qualities were evident both on and off the field. He was a vocal presence in the dressing room, and he was known for his ability to motivate his teammates and lead by example. He was also highly respected by his opponents, and his professionalism and sportsmanship were widely praised.

After retiring from playing in 2011, Vieira moved into coaching. He began his career as a youth coach at Manchester City, before moving on to become the head coach of New York City FC in 2016. In 2018, he took over as manager of French club OGC Nice, and he is currently in charge of Crystal Palace in the English Premier League.

Throughout his career, Vieira has demonstrated a commitment to leadership and a desire to make a positive impact on the teams he has been a part of. His playing career was marked by his physical and technical ability, as well as his tactical intelligence, and he was widely regarded as one of the best midfielders of his generation. As a coach, he has continued to develop his leadership qualities, and he is widely regarded as one of the most promising young managers in the game.

His approach to management and player development

Patrick Vieira is a former French footballer who played as a midfielder. He is now a coach, currently managing Crystal Palace in the English Premier League. Vieira's approach to management and player development is centered on a strong work ethic, communication, and building relationships with players.

As a player, Vieira was known for his physicality, technical ability, and leadership qualities. He won numerous trophies with Arsenal, including three Premier League titles and four FA Cups, as well as the 1998 World Cup and 2000 European Championship with the French national team. Vieira's success as a player provided him with a wealth of experience and knowledge that he has utilized in his coaching career.

Vieira's management approach focuses on building strong relationships with his players. He believes that communication is key to developing a successful team and places a strong emphasis on individual player development. Vieira is known for his meticulous approach to planning and preparation, and his attention to detail is evident in the tactical systems he employs on the field.

One of the key aspects of Vieira's management approach is his emphasis on a strong work ethic. He believes that hard work and dedication are essential to success in football, and he demands the same level of commitment from his players. Vieira's teams are known for their physicality and high press, which requires a great deal of energy and effort from all players on the field.

In terms of player development, Vieira is known for his ability to identify young talent and help them develop into top-level players. During his time at New York City FC, he helped develop several young players, including Jack Harrison and James Sands, who have gone on to become regular starters in MLS.

Case studies of Vieira's time at New York City FC and OGC Nice provide insight into his management approach. At New York City FC, Vieira was able to build a competitive team despite having a limited budget and a number of challenges, including a mid-season move to a new stadium. He was also successful in developing young players, as mentioned previously.

At OGC Nice, Vieira's team struggled initially, but he was able to turn things around by implementing a more attacking style of play and focusing on player development. He helped several players, including Youcef Atal and Allan

Saint-Maximin, reach new heights and earn moves to bigger clubs.

Lessons that can be learned from Vieira's management approach include the importance of communication and building strong relationships with players, the value of a strong work ethic and attention to detail, and the ability to identify and develop young talent. Vieira's success as a player and coach has earned him a reputation as one of the most promising young managers in the game, and his approach to management is sure to inspire and influence future generations of coaches.

Case studies of his time at New York City FC and OGC Nice

Patrick Vieira's time at New York City FC was his first experience managing a professional football team. He was appointed head coach in January 2016 and spent two and a half seasons at the club before leaving in June 2018. During his time in New York, Vieira focused on developing a playing style that was based on possession and quick transitions. He also placed a strong emphasis on player development, and many of the young players he brought through went on to establish themselves as regulars in the first team.

One of Vieira's most significant achievements at New York City FC was the development of Jack Harrison, a young winger who had been drafted by the club in the 2016 MLS SuperDraft. Under Vieira's guidance, Harrison developed into one of the most promising young players in the league and eventually earned a transfer to English Premier League side Manchester City. Vieira also oversaw the development of a number of other young players, including James Sands and Yangel Herrera, who went on to become important members of the New York City FC squad.

Vieira's tactical flexibility was also evident during his time at New York City FC. He experimented with a variety of formations and playing styles, depending on the strengths of his team and the weaknesses of his opponents. One notable example was his decision to switch to a three-man defense during the 2017 season, which helped the team to overcome a mid-season slump and finish in second place in the Eastern Conference.

After leaving New York City FC, Vieira was appointed as head coach of French Ligue 1 side OGC Nice in June 2018. His time at Nice was marked by some significant highs and lows, but his commitment to player development and tactical flexibility remained constant throughout his tenure.

In his first season at the club, Vieira guided Nice to a seventh-place finish in the league, their highest in four years. He achieved this by implementing a possession-based playing style and giving young players like Allan Saint-Maximin and Malang Sarr significant playing time. The following season, however, Vieira struggled to replicate this success, and the team finished in 12th place.

Despite this, Vieira continued to demonstrate his tactical flexibility, experimenting with a variety of formations and playing styles. In one notable example, he switched to a 3-5-2 formation midway through the 2019/20 season, which helped to shore up the team's defense and improve their overall performances.

Lessons that can be learned from Vieira's management approach

One of the key lessons that managers can learn from Patrick Vieira's approach is the importance of player development. Vieira has shown that by investing time and resources in developing young players, managers can create a team that is not only successful in the short term but also has a bright future ahead of it. This approach requires patience and a long-term vision, but it can pay significant dividends in the long run.

Another lesson that managers can learn from Vieira is the importance of tactical flexibility. By being willing to experiment with different formations and playing styles, managers can keep their opponents guessing and adapt to changing circumstances. This requires a deep understanding of the strengths and weaknesses of both your own team and your opponents, as well as the ability to make quick decisions and adjustments when necessary.

Finally, Vieira's emphasis on possession-based football is a lesson that managers at all levels of the game can learn from. By focusing on keeping the ball and controlling the tempo of the game, managers can create a team that is not only difficult to beat but also capable of dominating their opponents. This approach requires a high level of technical skill and discipline, but it can be highly effective when executed correctly.

Lessons that can be learned from Vieira's leadership style

Patrick Vieira is not only a successful player but also a promising manager with a distinct leadership style. Vieira's management approach is centered around building a strong team culture, emphasizing communication and creating a positive environment for his players. In this section, we will delve into the lessons that can be learned from Vieira's leadership style.

1. Creating a Strong Team Culture

One of the most significant lessons to be learned from Vieira's management approach is the importance of creating a strong team culture. In his various roles as a player and a manager, Vieira has been known for his leadership qualities and ability to bring people together. He places a great emphasis on the idea that a team must be built on a strong foundation of shared values and beliefs. Vieira understands that creating a positive team culture requires a concerted effort from everyone in the organization.

As a manager, Vieira has prioritized fostering a strong sense of team spirit. He is known for creating a welcoming and inclusive environment for players from diverse backgrounds, which has resulted in a more unified and cohesive team. By focusing on building a strong team culture, Vieira has been able to create a group of players who are more willing to work hard and support each other.

2. Emphasizing Communication

Another crucial aspect of Vieira's leadership style is his emphasis on communication. He recognizes that effective communication is essential to building a strong team culture and achieving success on the field. Vieira encourages open and honest communication between himself, his coaching staff, and his players. He makes a point of listening to his players' concerns and ideas and takes them into account when making decisions.

Vieira's approach to communication has resulted in a more transparent and collaborative team environment. By prioritizing communication, Vieira has been able to build trust and respect between himself and his players, which has led to a more positive and productive working relationship.

3. Creating a Positive Environment

Vieira is also known for creating a positive environment for his players. He understands that a team must be happy and motivated in order to perform at its best. Vieira's positive approach to management has led to a more enjoyable and satisfying experience for his players, which has translated into improved performances on the field.

Vieira's commitment to creating a positive environment extends beyond the field of play. He recognizes that his players are individuals with their own lives and concerns, and he takes an interest in their personal wellbeing. By showing a genuine interest in his players, Vieira has been able to build stronger relationships with them, which has resulted in a more loyal and committed team.

4. Leading by Example

Finally, one of the most important lessons to be learned from Vieira's leadership style is the importance of leading by example. Vieira is known for his strong work ethic and dedication to the game. He sets a high standard for himself and his players and expects nothing less than their best effort. By leading by example, Vieira has been able to inspire his players to work harder and strive for excellence.

Vieira's commitment to leading by example has also contributed to his credibility as a manager. His players respect him because they know that he has the same expectations for himself as he does for them. Vieira's willingness to roll up his sleeves and work alongside his players has created a more collaborative and productive team environment.

Conclusion

Patrick Vieira's leadership style is a testament to the importance of creating a strong team culture, emphasizing communication, and creating a positive environment for players. By prioritizing these aspects of management, Vieira has been able to build successful teams at both New York City FC and OGC Nice. His commitment to developing young players and experimenting with tactical systems is also a valuable lesson for managers at all levels of the game. Overall, Vieira's leadership style is a model for managers looking to build successful teams and develop talented players.

One of the key lessons that can be learned from Vieira's leadership style is the importance of creating a strong team culture. Vieira is known for his emphasis on team building and creating a positive environment for his players. He believes that a strong team culture is essential for success on the pitch, as it helps to foster a sense of unity and a common purpose among the players. This is evident in the way that he has brought together diverse groups of players from different backgrounds and nationalities at both New York City FC and OGC Nice.

Another important lesson from Vieira's leadership style is the importance of communication. Vieira is known for his open and honest communication with his players, and he encourages his players to communicate openly with each other as well. This helps to foster a sense of trust and transparency within the team, which is essential for building strong relationships and achieving success on the pitch.

Vieira also emphasizes the importance of creating a positive environment for his players. He believes that a positive atmosphere helps to keep players motivated and focused, and he works hard to create an environment in which his players feel supported and valued. This includes providing opportunities for players to develop their skills, as well as offering support and encouragement when they face challenges.

Finally, Vieira's commitment to developing young players and experimenting with tactical systems is also a valuable lesson for managers. By giving young players the opportunity to play significant roles in the first team, Vieira is able to develop their skills and help them reach their full potential. Additionally, by experimenting with different tactics and formations, Vieira is able to adapt his approach to suit the strengths and weaknesses of his team, which is essential for achieving success in a competitive environment.

Overall, Patrick Vieira's leadership style is a model for managers looking to build successful teams and develop talented players. By emphasizing the importance of team culture, communication, and creating a positive environment for players, Vieira has been able to achieve success both on and off the pitch.

Chapter 6: Mauricio Pochettino
Pochettino's playing career and early coaching experience

Mauricio Pochettino's playing career began in his hometown of Murphy, Argentina, where he started playing for a local team called Defensores de Murphy. In 1994, Pochettino moved to Newell's Old Boys, a well-known club in Argentina, where he made his professional debut. He quickly established himself as a reliable center-back and became an important member of the team that won the Clausura tournament in 1992.

In 1998, Pochettino was transferred to Spanish club Espanyol, where he spent the majority of his playing career. He quickly became a fan favorite due to his combative style of play and strong defensive skills. He also demonstrated his versatility by occasionally playing as a defensive midfielder.

During his time at Espanyol, Pochettino played in over 200 games and was named team captain in 2003. He is widely regarded as one of the club's greatest ever players, and his impact on the team was recognized in 2014 when he was inducted into the club's Hall of Fame.

Pochettino retired from playing in 2006 and immediately began his coaching career, starting out with Spanish lower league team, Palafrugell. In 2008, he returned to Espanyol as head coach, where he made an immediate impact. He guided the team to a surprise 10th place finish in La Liga in his first season in charge and followed that up with a successful campaign the following year, where the team finished in eighth place and reached the final of the Copa del Rey.

After leaving Espanyol in 2012, Pochettino took charge of English Premier League side Southampton. He led the team to a respectable eighth-place finish in his first season in charge, playing an attractive and attacking brand of football. His work at Southampton did not go unnoticed, and in 2014 he was appointed as manager of Tottenham Hotspur.

Pochettino's early coaching experience, coupled with his successful playing career, provided him with a strong foundation to become a successful manager. His understanding of the game, combined with his tactical knowledge and ability to inspire his players, has been key to his success in coaching.

His approach to team building and player development

Mauricio Pochettino is known for his ability to build successful teams by prioritizing team culture and player development. His approach to team building focuses on creating a positive and cohesive team environment that emphasizes hard work, discipline, and communication.

One of Pochettino's key strategies for team building is the creation of a strong team culture. He has spoken extensively about the importance of building relationships between players and creating a positive environment in the locker room. Pochettino emphasizes the importance of building a team that is united and focused on achieving its goals. He is known for organizing team bonding events and for encouraging players to spend time together off the pitch.

Pochettino is also known for his focus on player development. He has a reputation for giving young players an opportunity to play and for helping them to develop their skills. Pochettino has been credited with helping to develop a number of young players, including Harry Kane, Dele Alli, and Kyle Walker-Peters. He has a philosophy of giving young players a chance to prove themselves and of helping them to develop their skills through hard work and training.

Another key aspect of Pochettino's approach to team building is his emphasis on discipline and hard work. He is known for his rigorous training sessions and for his insistence on high standards from his players. Pochettino's approach is focused on creating a team that is physically and mentally strong, and that is able to perform at a high level for the entire duration of a match.

In terms of tactics, Pochettino's approach to team building is focused on a high-pressing, attacking style of play. His teams are known for their high-energy and aggressive style, with players pressing the opposition and looking to create chances through quick transitions. Pochettino has also been known to experiment with different formations and tactical systems, and is not afraid to make bold decisions in order to achieve success.

Overall, Pochettino's approach to team building and player development emphasizes the importance of a strong team culture, player development, discipline, hard work, and tactical flexibility. His success in building successful teams at Tottenham Hotspur and Paris Saint-Germain is a testament to the effectiveness of his management style.

Case studies of his time at Espanyol, Southampton, and Tottenham Hotspur

Mauricio Pochettino is widely regarded as one of the best managers in modern football, and his success at Espanyol, Southampton, and Tottenham Hotspur provides a wealth of case studies that highlight his approach to management and leadership.

At Espanyol, Pochettino inherited a struggling team and set about rebuilding the club from the ground up. He prioritized the development of young players and implemented a pressing style of play that quickly became a hallmark of his teams. Pochettino also emphasized the importance of team culture and instilled a strong sense of unity and camaraderie within the squad. Despite a limited budget and few resources, Pochettino was able to guide Espanyol to mid-table finishes and established them as a competitive force in La Liga.

Pochettino's success at Espanyol caught the attention of Southampton, who hired him as their new manager in 2013. At Southampton, Pochettino continued his focus on player development and team culture, but also demonstrated his ability to adapt to the demands of the Premier League. He implemented a high-pressing, possession-based style of play that proved effective against the league's top teams, and also invested in the recruitment of talented young players such as Nathaniel Clyne, Dejan Lovren, and Sadio Mane. Under Pochettino's guidance, Southampton finished eighth in the Premier League, their highest finish in over a decade.

Pochettino's success at Southampton led to his appointment as manager of Tottenham Hotspur in 2014. At Tottenham, Pochettino continued to emphasize the development of young players and the importance of team culture. He also implemented a high-pressing, possession-based style of play that quickly became synonymous with his teams. Pochettino's impact at Tottenham was immediate, as he guided the club to a fifth-place finish in his first season in charge. He then led Tottenham to back-to-back top-four finishes, culminating in a runners-up spot in the 2016/17 season.

Perhaps Pochettino's greatest achievement at Tottenham, however, was his ability to build a team that challenged for major honors despite limited resources. He developed a number of young players such as Harry Kane, Dele Alli, and Eric Dier into top-level performers, while also making shrewd signings such as Toby Alderweireld, Kieran Trippier, and Heung-min Son. Pochettino's ability to get the most out of his players and build a cohesive team was evident in Tottenham's memorable run to the UEFA Champions League final in 2019.

Overall, Pochettino's case studies at Espanyol, Southampton, and Tottenham highlight his ability to develop young players, create a strong team culture, and implement a high-pressing, possession-based style of play. His success at all three clubs is a testament to his tactical acumen and leadership qualities, and provides valuable lessons for managers at all levels of the game.

Lessons that can be learned from Pochettino's management approach

Mauricio Pochettino is a highly regarded manager who is known for his unique approach to management and his ability to build successful teams. Through his experience at Espanyol, Southampton, and Tottenham Hotspur, there are several lessons that can be learned from his management approach.

1. Importance of team culture and identity

Pochettino is a firm believer in the importance of establishing a strong team culture and identity. He believes that having a clear vision for the team and establishing a positive team culture is essential for building a successful team. This is evident in his time at Tottenham, where he created a team that was known for its high-pressing and aggressive style of play.

2. Emphasis on player development

Another key aspect of Pochettino's management approach is his emphasis on player development. He is committed to giving young players an opportunity to play and develop, as evidenced by his successful development of players such as Harry Kane, Dele Alli, and Kyle Walker-Peters. He also places a high value on the mental and emotional development of players, working closely with them to ensure that they are able to cope with the pressures of professional football.

3. Tactical flexibility

Pochettino is known for his tactical flexibility and willingness to adapt his tactics based on the opposition and the situation. He is not afraid to experiment with different formations and systems, as evidenced by his use of a back three during Tottenham's 2016/17 campaign. This willingness to adapt and experiment has been a key factor in his success as a manager.

4. Importance of communication

Communication is another key aspect of Pochettino's management approach. He places a high value on clear communication with his players, staff, and the media. He is known for his open and honest communication style, which has helped to build trust and respect with his players and staff.

5. Long-term planning

Finally, Pochettino is a manager who believes in long-term planning. He has a clear vision for the future of his teams and works closely with his staff and players to ensure that they are all working towards the same goals. This long-term planning has been a key factor in his success, as evidenced by his ability to guide Tottenham to the Champions League final in 2019.

Overall, there are several lessons that can be learned from Pochettino's management approach. His emphasis on team culture and identity, player development, tactical flexibility, communication, and long-term planning are all valuable lessons for managers at all levels of the game. By following these principles, managers can build successful teams and create a positive environment for their players to thrive in.

Chapter 7: Casey Stoney

Stoney's playing career and early coaching experience

Casey Stoney is a former English footballer who played as a defender for various teams during her career, including Arsenal, Chelsea, Lincoln Ladies, and Liverpool. She made her debut for the England national team in 2000 and went on to earn 130 caps, serving as the team's captain for a period of time.

Stoney's playing career began at Chelsea in 1998, where she played for two seasons before moving to Arsenal. She spent the majority of her career at Arsenal, where she won numerous titles including the FA Women's Cup, the FA Women's Premier League, and the UEFA Women's Cup. She also had a brief stint in the United States with Sky Blue FC in 2009.

After retiring from playing in 2018, Stoney turned to coaching and quickly made a name for herself in the women's game. She began her coaching career as an assistant coach at Arsenal Women under Pedro Martinez Losa. She then took on a role as the head coach of the newly-formed Liverpool Women's team in 2018, where she helped guide the team to a fourth-place finish in the FA Women's Super League.

In 2018, Stoney was appointed as the head coach of Manchester United Women, who were preparing for their inaugural season in the FA Women's Championship. In her first season in charge, Stoney led the team to promotion to the FA Women's Super League, finishing top of the table with 18 wins from 20 matches.

Throughout her playing career, Stoney was known for her leadership qualities both on and off the pitch. She was a vocal and commanding presence at the back and was often called upon to lead her teams both on and off the pitch. Her experience as a player has undoubtedly helped shape her approach to coaching and leadership.

Stoney's early coaching experience was heavily influenced by her time as an assistant coach at Arsenal Women. Under Losa, she learned the importance of developing a playing style and philosophy that suits the team's strengths and allows them to play to their full potential. She also learned the importance of attention to detail and meticulous planning, something that has become a hallmark of her coaching style.

Stoney's approach to team building and player development is heavily centered on creating a positive and supportive team culture. She places a strong emphasis on building relationships with her players and creating a safe and inclusive environment in which they can thrive. This approach has been particularly important for Stoney, who has been an advocate for greater diversity and inclusion in the women's game.

Stoney's coaching philosophy is focused on developing players who are technically proficient, tactically aware, and mentally resilient. She places a strong emphasis on individual development, ensuring that each player receives the support and guidance they need to reach their full potential. She is also known for her tactical flexibility, regularly changing formations and tactics to suit the opposition and the strengths of her own team.

Throughout her coaching career, Stoney has demonstrated a willingness to take risks and make bold decisions. This was particularly evident during her time at Manchester United Women, where she was tasked with building a team from scratch. She was unafraid to give young players a chance and was willing to experiment with different formations and tactics until she found a winning formula.

Overall, Stoney's approach to coaching and leadership is characterized by her commitment to creating a positive and inclusive team culture, her emphasis on individual development, and her tactical flexibility. Her success at Manchester United Women is a testament to the effectiveness of her approach and the impact it can have on a team's performance.

Her approach to team building and player development

Casey Stoney's approach to team building and player development is rooted in her philosophy of building a strong team culture that values hard work, discipline, and accountability. Stoney believes in empowering her players and giving them a voice in the team's decision-making process, which has helped to foster a sense of ownership and responsibility among her players.

One of the key aspects of Stoney's management style is her commitment to developing young players. She has created a pathway for young players to progress from the academy to the first team, with several players making their professional debuts under her guidance. Stoney also places a strong emphasis on player development, working closely with her coaching staff to create individualized training programs for each player.

In addition to developing players on the field, Stoney also prioritizes their personal development. She encourages her players to be active in the community and to use their platform to make a positive impact. Under her leadership, Manchester United Women have undertaken several initiatives to give back to the community, including visiting local schools and hospitals and partnering with local charities.

Stoney's approach to team building is also focused on creating a positive and inclusive environment for her players. She has been vocal about the need to increase diversity and representation in the sport and has been a vocal advocate for LGBTQ+ rights. Stoney has worked to create a team culture that values diversity and inclusivity, and her team has been recognized for its commitment to these values both on and off the field.

Another aspect of Stoney's management style is her tactical flexibility. She is willing to adapt her team's tactics to fit the strengths and weaknesses of her players, and she is not afraid to experiment with different formations and systems. This approach has helped Manchester United Women to be successful in multiple competitions, including reaching the Women's Super League for the first time in their history.

Overall, Stoney's approach to team building and player development emphasizes the importance of creating a strong team culture, developing young players, and prioritizing personal and community development. Her commitment to diversity and inclusivity in the sport has made her a role model for young players and coaches alike.

Case studies of her time at Manchester United Women

Case studies of Casey Stoney's time at Manchester United Women provide valuable insights into her approach to management and the success she has achieved in her short tenure. Stoney was appointed as the manager of Manchester United Women in June 2018, and in just three years, she has led the team to two promotions and a fourth-place finish in their debut season in the Women's Super League. Here are some case studies of her time at Manchester United Women:

1. Building a winning team culture

One of the key factors that have contributed to Manchester United Women's success under Stoney is the strong team culture that she has built. Stoney places a great emphasis on creating a positive and supportive environment for her players, which helps them to perform at their best. She has been instrumental in creating a culture of togetherness and resilience that has helped the team to overcome setbacks and bounce back from defeats.

Stoney has also placed a great emphasis on player development, particularly for young players. She has given young players significant playing time, which has allowed them to gain valuable experience and develop their skills. This approach has helped to create a team that is not only successful in the short term but also has a bright future ahead.

2. Tactical flexibility

Stoney's tactical flexibility has been another key factor in Manchester United Women's success. She is not afraid to experiment with different formations and systems depending on the opposition and the situation. This approach has helped the team to be adaptable and able to react to different situations.

In the 2019/2020 season, Stoney adopted a 4-3-3 formation, which allowed her team to play a more attacking style of football. This approach proved to be successful, as Manchester United Women finished the season as champions of the Women's Championship.

3. Creating a sense of community

Stoney has placed a great emphasis on creating a sense of community around the team. She has worked closely with the Manchester United Foundation to engage with local schools and communities, which has helped to build a strong relationship between the team and its supporters.

She has also been vocal in her support of women's football and has been an advocate for greater investment and support for the sport. This approach has helped to create a positive image for Manchester United Women and has contributed to their success on and off the pitch.

4. Empowering players

Stoney's approach to management involves empowering players to take ownership of their own development and performance. She encourages her players to take responsibility for their actions and to take an active role in the team's success.

This approach has been particularly effective with Manchester United Women's captain, Katie Zelem, who has thrived under Stoney's leadership. Zelem has been given the freedom to express herself on the pitch and has developed into one of the best midfielders in the Women's Super League.

Overall, Casey Stoney's time at Manchester United Women provides valuable case studies of her approach to management and player development. Her emphasis on creating a strong team culture, tactical flexibility, community engagement, and player empowerment has contributed to the team's success on and off the pitch.

Lessons that can be learned from Stoney's management approach

Casey Stoney's management approach is characterized by her focus on building a strong team culture, developing players, and empowering them to take ownership of their performance. There are several key lessons that can be learned from her management approach.

1. Building a strong team culture: Stoney understands the importance of building a strong team culture that fosters trust, communication, and collaboration. She has created an environment where players feel comfortable expressing themselves and taking ownership of their performance. This has led to a strong sense of camaraderie and a willingness to work hard for each other.

2. Developing players: Stoney places a strong emphasis on player development, both on and off the field. She creates a personalized development plan for each player, focusing on their strengths and weaknesses, and sets clear goals for them to work towards. She also creates opportunities for players to develop their leadership skills and take on more responsibility within the team.

3. Empowering players: Stoney believes in empowering players to take ownership of their performance and make decisions on the field. She encourages players to

take risks and be creative, while also holding them accountable for their actions. This has led to a more dynamic and fluid playing style, as players are encouraged to take initiative and play to their strengths.

4. Attention to detail: Stoney is known for her meticulous attention to detail, both in training and in matches. She analyzes opponents thoroughly and creates a game plan tailored to their strengths and weaknesses. She also pays close attention to the physical and mental well-being of her players, ensuring that they are well-rested and prepared for each match.

5. Creating a positive environment: Stoney understands the importance of creating a positive environment for her players, both on and off the field. She encourages players to have fun and enjoy themselves, while also fostering a strong work ethic and a culture of professionalism. This has created a team that is both successful and enjoyable to be a part of.

In conclusion, Casey Stoney's management approach is characterized by her focus on building a strong team culture, developing players, empowering them to take ownership of their performance, attention to detail, and creating a positive environment. These are valuable lessons that can be applied to management at all levels of the game, and can help to create successful, cohesive teams.

Conclusion
The key qualities of successful football leaders and managers

Football leadership and management are multifaceted and complex fields that require a range of skills, qualities, and traits. Successful leaders and managers must possess a unique combination of strategic thinking, tactical acumen, emotional intelligence, communication skills, and a deep understanding of the game.

One key quality that all successful football leaders and managers possess is the ability to build strong relationships with their players. This involves creating a culture of trust, honesty, and respect, as well as taking the time to understand each player's individual needs and motivations. A manager who can foster positive relationships with their players is more likely to inspire loyalty and commitment, which can translate into improved on-field performance.

Another key quality of successful football leaders and managers is their ability to create and implement effective game plans. This requires a deep understanding of the game, including its tactical nuances, and the ability to identify and exploit weaknesses in the opposition. Managers who can create effective game plans are more likely to succeed on the field, and their teams will be better prepared to deal with the challenges of modern football.

Successful football leaders and managers are also highly adaptable and flexible. They are willing to experiment with different tactics, formations, and strategies, and they are not afraid to make changes in response to changing circumstances. This requires a willingness to take risks and try new things, as well as the ability to think creatively and outside the box.

Another key quality of successful football leaders and managers is their ability to develop and nurture young talent. This involves identifying and recruiting promising young players, as well as providing them with the support and guidance they need to reach their full potential. Managers who can develop young talent are more likely to build successful teams over the long term, as they will have a strong pipeline of players to draw upon.

Finally, successful football leaders and managers must possess strong communication skills. They must be able to effectively communicate their vision and strategy to their players, as well as motivate and inspire them to achieve their goals. This requires a combination of verbal and nonverbal communication skills, as well as the ability to read and interpret body language.

In conclusion, successful football leadership and management require a range of skills, qualities, and traits. The ability to build strong relationships with players, create and implement effective game plans, be adaptable and flexible, develop young talent, and possess strong communication skills are all key to success in the modern game. While each manager and leader will have their own unique approach, these qualities can serve as a blueprint for success at all levels of the game.

The importance of adaptability and innovation in modern football

In the world of modern football, adaptability and innovation are two essential qualities that successful leaders and managers possess. As the game continues to evolve, those who fail to adapt and innovate risk being left behind. In this concluding section, we will explore the importance of these two qualities in modern football management and the benefits they bring to a team.

Adaptability is a key trait that successful football managers possess. The ability to adapt to changing situations, whether it be tactical changes, injuries, or changes in player personnel, is essential to success. Football is a game that is constantly evolving, and managers who are able to adapt to these changes are more likely to succeed than those who are not. Managers who are adaptable are able to make quick decisions and adjust their tactics to counter their opponents, which can make all the difference in a game.

One example of a manager who has shown adaptability is Pep Guardiola. Guardiola is known for his tactical flexibility and his ability to change his tactics based on his opponent's strengths and weaknesses. This adaptability has helped him achieve success at every club he has managed. At Barcelona, he played a possession-based style of football that relied on quick passing and movement, while at Bayern Munich, he used a more direct approach that focused on counter-attacking. At Manchester City, he has again adapted his tactics to suit his team's strengths and weaknesses, which has led to great success in recent years.

In addition to adaptability, innovation is another key trait that successful football managers possess. Innovation involves coming up with new and creative ideas to improve the team's performance. This can involve everything from developing new training techniques to using new technology to gain a competitive advantage. Innovation is important because it allows a team to stay ahead of its competitors and achieve success in a rapidly evolving game.

One example of a manager who has shown innovation is Jurgen Klopp. Klopp is known for his high-energy, pressing style of football, which has been adopted by many teams around the world. Klopp's use of technology to improve his team's performance is also innovative. For example, Liverpool has invested in a state-of-the-art training ground that includes a hydrotherapy pool, a sports science laboratory, and a dedicated recovery area. This investment in technology has helped the team stay ahead of its competitors and maintain its high levels of performance.

Innovation can also involve taking risks and trying new things. Managers who are willing to take risks and experiment with new tactics or formations are more likely to achieve success than those who play it safe. For example, Antonio Conte's use of a back-three formation during his time at Chelsea was a bold move that paid off. The formation allowed Chelsea to dominate games and win the Premier League title in his first season in charge.

In conclusion, adaptability and innovation are two key qualities that successful football managers possess. The ability to adapt to changing situations and innovate new ideas is essential in the modern game, where teams are constantly evolving and looking for new ways to gain a competitive advantage. Managers who possess these qualities are more likely to achieve success and lead their teams to glory. As football continues to evolve, it will be interesting to see which managers can adapt and innovate to stay ahead of the game.

Final thoughts and recommendations for aspiring managers and coaches

As we have explored throughout this book, successful football managers and coaches possess a wide range of qualities that contribute to their ability to lead their teams to victory. From the tactical genius of Pep Guardiola to the motivational skills of Jurgen Klopp, it is clear that there is no one-size-fits-all approach to management in football. However, there are certain key qualities that seem to be common among successful managers, and aspiring coaches can learn from these qualities to develop their own style of management.

One of the most important qualities of successful football managers is the ability to adapt to changing circumstances. The game of football is constantly evolving, and managers who are unable to adapt their tactics and strategies to keep up with these changes will quickly fall behind. This is particularly true in today's game, where the use of data analytics and technology is becoming increasingly important. Successful managers must be able to incorporate these tools into their decision-making process, while also maintaining the human element that makes football such a beautiful game.

Another important quality of successful football managers is innovation. The best managers are always looking for new ways to gain an edge over their opponents, whether it be through new tactical systems, unique training methods, or innovative ways of motivating their players. Innovation requires a willingness to take risks and experiment, and not every idea will be successful. However, managers who are able to successfully innovate can gain a significant advantage over their competitors and lead their teams to greater success.

In addition to adaptability and innovation, successful football managers must also possess strong leadership skills. This includes the ability to build a strong team culture, communicate effectively with players and staff, and create a positive environment for their team to thrive. Managers who are able to establish a culture of hard work, dedication, and teamwork will be able to get the most out of their players and build a team that is greater than the sum of its parts.

Aspiring managers and coaches can learn a great deal from the successful managers we have examined in this book. However, it is important to remember that there is no one-size-fits-all approach to management in football. The best managers are those who are able to adapt their approach to their specific team and circumstances, while also maintaining a commitment to the key qualities that contribute to success.

If you are an aspiring manager or coach, here are a few recommendations to help you develop your skills and achieve success in the game:

1. Continuously educate yourself: The game of football is constantly evolving, and it is important to stay up-to-date on the latest trends and strategies. Attend coaching courses, read books and articles, and watch games to gain a deeper understanding of the game.

2. Build strong relationships: As a manager, you will be working closely with players, staff, and other stakeholders. Building strong relationships based on trust, respect, and communication is crucial to your success.

3. Be adaptable: The game of football is unpredictable, and the best managers are those who are able to adapt their tactics and strategies to changing circumstances.

4. Be innovative: Don't be afraid to try new things and take risks. Innovation can be the key to gaining a competitive advantage and achieving success.

5. Stay focused on your goals: Set clear goals for yourself and your team, and stay focused on achieving them. Remember that success in football is a marathon, not a sprint.

In conclusion, the world of football management is a complex and ever-changing landscape. Successful managers possess a wide range of qualities, including adaptability, innovation, and strong leadership skills. By learning from the experiences of successful managers like Pep Guardiola, Jurgen Klopp, Patrick Vieira, Mauricio Pochettino, and Casey Stoney, aspiring coaches and managers can develop their own style of management and achieve success in the game.

Key Terms and Definitions

To help you better understand the language and concepts related to aging and older adults, below you will find a list of key terms and their definitions.

1. Management: The process of planning, organizing, leading, and controlling resources in order to achieve organizational goals.

2. Leadership: The ability to inspire, influence, and guide others towards a common goal or vision.

3. Player development: The process of training and nurturing players to improve their skills, knowledge, and performance on the field.

4. Tactical flexibility: The ability to adapt and change tactical systems and strategies depending on the situation and opponent.

5. Team culture: The shared values, attitudes, beliefs, and behaviors that shape the identity of a team.

6. Communication: The exchange of information, ideas, and feedback between individuals or groups.

7. Positive environment: A supportive and encouraging atmosphere that promotes teamwork, learning, and growth.

8. Adaptability: The ability to adjust and respond to changing circumstances, situations, or environments.

9. Innovation: The introduction of new ideas, methods, or technologies to improve performance or achieve a competitive advantage.

10. Strategy: A plan or approach designed to achieve a specific goal or objective, often involving a combination of tactics, resources, and actions.

11. Vision: A clear and inspiring picture of the future that guides decision-making, planning, and action.

12. Motivation: The drive, energy, and enthusiasm that propels individuals or teams towards a goal or objective.

13. Performance: The level of achievement or success in completing tasks, goals, or objectives.

14. Success: The achievement of desired goals or outcomes, often involving a combination of factors such as hard work, talent, skill, strategy, and luck.

15. Professionalism: The quality of conduct, behavior, and performance expected of individuals in a particular profession, often involving a combination of ethics, standards, and values..

Supporting Materials

Introduction:

- Grant, J. (2016). The manager: Inside the minds of football's leaders. Bloomsbury Publishing.

Chapter 1: Roy Keane

- Keane, R. (2014). The second half. Weidenfeld & Nicolson.
- Brady, A. (2014). The authorized biography: Red. John Blake.

Chapter 2: Rafael Benitez

- Benitez, R. (2013). Champions league dreams: Rafael Benitez. Transworld Publishers.
- Guillem Balague (2018). Rafa Benitez: The biography. Orion Publishing Group.

Chapter 3: Marcelo Bielsa

- Wilson, J. (2019). The names heard long ago: How Marcelo Bielsa inspired a football generation. Bloomsbury Publishing.
- Zeng, X. (2020). Marcelo Bielsa: The Performance Analysis. eBookIt. com.

Chapter 4: Emma Hayes

- Hayes, E. (2021). Dare to be different: A women's football memoir. Yellow Jersey.
- Bate, A. (2020). The women's football handbook. Pitch Publishing.

Chapter 5: Patrick Vieira

- Vieira, P. (2018). Patrick Vieira: My life in red and white. Orion Publishing Group.
- Collyer, D. (2021). Patrick Vieira: The biography. The History Press.

Chapter 6: Mauricio Pochettino

- Pochettino, M. (2021). Brave new world: Inside Pochettino's Spurs. Orion Publishing Group.
- Balague, G. (2017). Brave new world: Inside Pochettino's Spurs. Weidenfeld & Nicolson.

Chapter 7: Casey Stoney

- Stoney, C. (2022). Changing the game: The Casey Stoney story. HarperCollins.
- Caudwell, J. (2020). Women's football in the UK: Continuing with gender analyses. Palgrave Macmillan.

Conclusion:

- Cox, M. (2020). The mixer: The story of Premier League tactics, from route one to false nines. HarperCollins.
- Kerr, J. (2020). Legacy: What the All Blacks can teach us about the business of life. Constable.

www.ingramcontent.com/pod-product-compliance
Lightning Source LLC
LaVergne TN
LVHW012121070526
838202LV00056B/5822